Portrait of a Lady

Quilts for a Woman's Journey Through Life

Christina McCourt

Portrait of a Lady –
Quilts for a Woman's Journey Through Life
By Christina McCourt

Editor: Kent Richards
Technical Editor: Deanna Hodson
Book Design: Sarah Mosher
Photography: Aaron Leimkuehler
Illustration: Lon Eric Craven
Production Assistance: Jo Ann Groves

Published by:
Kansas City Star Books
1729 Grand Blvd.
Kansas City, Missouri, USA 64108

First edition, first printing
978-1-61169-081-1

Library of Congress Control Number:
2012956495

Printed in the United States of America
by Walsworth Publishing Co., Marceline, MO
To order copies, call StarInfo at
(816) 234-4242 and say "Operator"

Walsworth

The Quilter's Home Page

KANSAS CITY STAR
QUILTS
Continuing the Tradition

Table of Contents

*My grandmother, Alma Lucille,
as a young woman.*

Acknowledgements

I would like to thank the following people for their help:

My family first and foremost!

Moda Fabric for the *Cattails and Clover* and *Sandhill Plum*s by Kansas Troubles Quilters fabric lines.

Windham Fabric for the *General's Wives* by Nancy Gere fabric line.

Marcus Fabrics for the *Cocheco Mills* fabric.

Gina Janes for machine quilting *Portrait of a Lady*, *Auntie's Bed Quilt* and *Love and Home Wall Hanging*.

Carla Gower for machine quilting *Nanny's Table Runner*, *Mother's Throw* and *Bouquet of Bridal Flowers*.

I would also like to thank my Kansas City Star production team:

My editor Kent Richards
My book designer Sarah Mosher
My illustrator Lon Eric Craven
My technical editor Deanna Hodson
My production assistant Jo Ann Groves
My photographer Aaron Leimkuehler

A great big thank you to Diane McLendon and Doug Weaver for giving me the opportunity to publish *Portrait of a Lady*.

I would also like to express my gratitude to the Missouri Department of Natural Resources and Janae Fuller for allowing us the use of the Battle of Lexington State Historic Site for the photography. Many thanks to Edie McGinnis and Teresa for their assistance at the photo shoot. For more information on the Battle of Lexington State Historic Site visit: http://mostateparks.com/park/battle-lexington-state-historic-site.

MISSOURI
STATE PARKS

About the Author

Christina McCourt grew up in the small town of New London in northeast Missouri. Christina still resides in New London, just one block from her childhood home. She makes her home with her husband Shawn, 4 children (Andrew, Melanie, Brendan and Drake), 4 dogs and 3 cats. In addition to designing quilts, she's also a substitute teacher for the local school district.

Christina grew up watching her grandmother, Irene, and mother, Belinda, making quilts and other craft projects. The quilting bug didn't hit Christina until 2001 and then it was quite by accident. Christina asked for a sewing machine for her birthday with the intention of making dresses for her pre-school daughter. She quickly found out that she didn't have the skills to make clothes, so she decided to try making a quilt. It was a small Irish chain quilt and although it was nowhere near perfect, she's still proud of that first quilt. Her grandmother, Irene, quilted it for her on her mid-arm quilting machine. Encouraged by her first effort, Christina learned from her mistakes and continued to grow in her quilt-making abilities.

In 2008 she had bought some fabric and could not find a pattern she liked to go with it. So she sat down and designed a quilt using old-fashioned pencil and paper. She has since abandoned that method and now uses EQ7 to design her quilts. In the spring of 2009, she was approached by Pat Waelder of the Hickory Stick Gift and Quilt Shop to design a quilt to be raffled off for the Tom and Becky Program in Hannibal, Missouri. The quilt was made using the *Mark Twain* fabric by Windham Fabrics. This was the official start of her quilt designing career.

In the beginning, Christina designed and sold patterns exclusively at the Hickory Stick shop. In 2009 she approached Nancy Dill at Quiltwoman.com to publish her patterns and has been with them ever since. Christina has been published in numerous magazines including: *Quilt, Quilt Sampler, Fabric Trends, Quilting for Christmas, Quilt Almanac, Quiltmaker's 100 Blocks* and *Fons and Porter's Scrap Quilts*.

Christina hopes to be designing quilts for many years to come! Visit her at: www.cmccourtquiltdesigns.com.

Introduction

I created *Portrait of a Lady* because I wanted a quilt that showed the natural progression of a lady through her life's journey. I thought about my grandmother, Alma Lucille. Looking through pictures you can see who she was at different times in her life. And those people in the pictures had different relationships with her. From baby daughter to bride to mother to grandmother and everything in between. She played so many roles.

Before you can be a lady, you must first be a *baby*. I chose the *Baby Bunting* block to represent the beginning of a her life.

Of course when a lady is born she becomes a *daughter*. The *Farmer's Daughter* block seemed like the perfect choice for this role.

A lady may or may not become a *sister*. I chose the *Sister's Choice* block to represent this aspect of her life. Alma loved her sisters and cherished their relationships.

As a *school girl*, a young lady prepares for life ahead. I chose the *School Girl* block for this important part of growing up.

If a lady is a sister, she just might become an *aunt*. I chose the *Aunt's Favorite* block to represent this part of a lady's life.

A lady most certainly dreams of being a *bride* one day. The *Bride's Bouquet* block was an easy choice for this life changing role.

Once a lady becomes a bride, her next role will hopefully be that of a *mother*. I chose the *Mother's Choice* block for the most important role of all.

Once a lady's children are grown, she will hopefully be blessed with grandchildren and earn the title of *grandmother*. I chose the *Grandmother's Cross* block to symbolize this special relationship.

Of course a lady's life would not be complete without a *house* and *love*. For that, I picked the Home and Heart blocks.

In making the *Portrait of a Lady* quilt, you will follow the path of a lovely, lovely lady named Alma Lucille.

Enjoy!

Alma's daughter, Belinda, remembers:
"Mom always liked to laugh and sing.
She was beautiful inside and out."

I never knew who I was going to wake up with in my bed because Alma was always bringing friends home for the night."

– Alma's sister, Olive

SCHOOL GIRL

Cutting Instructions:

From the orange fabric, cut:
1 – 4⅞" square, cut once on the diagonal

From the blue fabric, cut:
1 – 2⅞" square

From the green fabric, cut:
2 – 2⅞" squares

From the light fabric, cut:
5 – 2⅞" squares
4 – 2½" squares

9. Sew a 4 flying geese unit to the bottom of the block. Press the seam toward the geese unit.

10. Sew a 6 flying geese unit to the previous unit. Press the seam toward the geese unit. Square to 12½".

Sewing the Block:

1. Cut 2 – 2⅞" light squares in half on the diagonal once. Draw a line on the diagonal of the remaining 3. Putting right sides together, match a 2⅞" light square and a 2⅞" blue square. Sew ¼" on both sides of the drawn line. Cut apart on the line. Press the seam toward the blue. Square to 2½". Make 2. Repeat with the remaining light squares and 2 green squares to make 4 more units.

2. Sew 2 light triangles to the sides of the blue unit from step 1. Press the seams toward the light. Make 2.

3. Sew a 4⅞" orange triangle to the previous unit. Press the seam toward the orange. Square to 4½". Make 2.

4. Sew a 2½" light square and a green unit from step 1 together. Press the seam toward the light. Make 4.

5. Sew 2 units together from step 4 to make a square. Refer to diagram below. Press the seam to one side. Square to 4½". Make 2.

6. Sew a unit from step 3 and a unit from step 5 together to form a row. Press the seam toward the orange. Make 2.

7. Sew the 2 rows together to form a block. Press the seam to one side. Square to 8½".

8. Sew a 4 flying geese unit to the bottom of the block. Press the seam toward the geese unit.

9. Sew a 6 flying geese unit to the previous unit. Press the seam toward the geese unit. Square to 12½".

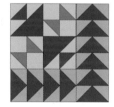

AUNT'S FAVORITE

Cutting Instructions:

From the orange fabric, cut:
1 – 2⅝" square

From the blue fabric, cut:
1 – 2⅝" square

From the red fabric, cut:
1 – 4⅜" square, cut once on the diagonal

From the brown fabric, cut:
1 – 4⅜" square, cut once on the diagonal

From the green fabric, cut:
4 – 1½" × 2¼" rectangles
1 – 1½" square

From the light fabric, cut:
4 – 1½" × 2¼" rectangles
6 – 2⅝" squares

Alma played French horn in the high school marching band. A gifted musician, Alma's granddaughter, Emily remembers: "I loved sitting beside her and playing the organ for hours on end."

Sewing the Block:

1. Draw a line on the diagonal of 2 – 2⅝" light squares. Cut once on the diagonal the remaining 4 – 2⅝" light squares.

2. Putting right sides together, match a 2⅝" light square with a 2⅝" orange square. Sew ¼" on both sides of the drawn line. Cut apart on the drawn line. Press the seam toward the orange. Square to 2¼". Repeat with the blue square. Make 2 of each.

3. Sew 2 light triangles to the sides of the units from step 2. Press the seams toward the light.

4. Sew a red triangle to the blue units from step 3. Press the seam toward the red. Square to 4". Repeat with brown and orange units.

5. Sew a 1½" × 2¼" light rectangle and a 1½" × 2¼" green rectangle together. Press the seam toward the green. Make 4.

6. Sew 2 units from step 4 and a unit from step 5 together to form a row. Press the seam toward the center. Make 2.

7. Sew 2 units from step 5 to two sides of a 1½" green square to make a row. Press the seams toward the light.

"Nanny made the best mashed potatoes ever!
Nobody can make them like her."

— Alma's granddaughter, Emily

8. Sew 2 rows from step 6 and a row from step 7 together to form the block. Press the seams toward the center. Square to 8½".

9. Sew a 4 flying geese unit to the bottom of the block. Press the seam toward the geese unit.

10. Sew a 6 flying geese unit to the previous unit. Press the seam toward the geese unit. Square to 12½".

BRIDE'S BOUQUET

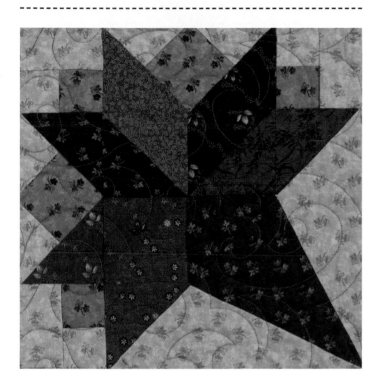

Cutting Instructions:

From the gold fabric, cut:
3 – 2" squares B
2 – 2⅝" squares D

From EACH of 2 green, red, and orange fabrics, cut:
1 – 3⅞" square, cut once on the diagonal, F, G, H, I, J, K

From the brown fabric, cut:
1 – 3⅞" square, cut once on the diagonal, L Top
1 – 4⅞" × 7⅜" rectangle, L Base

From the light fabric, cut:
3 – 2" squares A
3 – 2" × 3½" rectangles C
1 – 4¼" square, cut twice on the diagonal E
2 – 3½" × 10⅝" rectangles M

Sewing the Block:

1. Sew a 2" gold square B and a 2" light square A together. Press the seam toward the gold. Make 3.

2. Sew the units from step 1 and 2" × 3½" light rectangles C together. Press the seam toward the light. Square to 3½".

3. Sew a light triangle E to 2 adjacent sides of a 2⅝" gold square D. Press the seams toward the light. Make 2.

4. Sew a red triangle F to the right side of the unit from step 3. Press the seam toward the red. Repeat with red triangle H.

5. Sew a green triangle G to the left side of the previous unit. Press the seam toward the green. Repeat with green triangle I to the unit with red triangle H.

6. Sew 2 units from step 2 and the F/G unit from step 5 together to form a row. Press the seams toward the center.

7. Sew a unit from step 2 and the H/I unit from step 5 together to form a row. Press the seam away from the square unit.

8. Sew a red triangle H and a green triangle G together. Sew a green triangle I and an orange triangle J together. Sew an orange triangle K and a red triangle F together. Press the seams open.

9. Sew a green/red unit H/G, and a red/orange unit F/K from step 8 and an orange triangle K together as in the diagram below.

10. Sew a green/orange unit I/J from step 8, an orange triangle J and a brown triangle L together as in the diagram below. Press the seams toward the triangles.

11. Sew the units from steps 9 and 10 together. Press seam toward the triangle unit.

12. On the brown 4⅞" × 7⅜" rectangle L, mark the center on one of the 4⅞" sides. From that mark cut diagonally to the corners.

13. Put the 2 – 3½" × 10⅝" light rectangles M wrong sides together. Along the 10⅝" side mark 3½" in. From that mark cut diagonally to the corners.

14. Using a scant ¼" seam allowance, sew the cut pieces from steps 12 and 13 together. Press the seams toward the light.

15. Sew the units from steps 11 and 14 together. Press the seam toward the flower base. Square to 9½".

16. Sew the units from steps 7 and 15 together. Press the seam away from the center.

17. Sew the units from steps 6 and 16 together. Press the seam toward the center. Square to 12½".

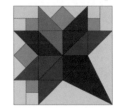

Alma as a young bride.

MOTHER'S CHOICE

Cutting Instructions:

From the light fabric, cut:
1 – 6¼" square, cut twice on the diagonal
6 – 2⅜" squares
4 – 3⅞" squares, cut once on the diagonal

From the brown fabric, cut:
2 – 2⅜" squares

From the gold fabric, cut:
2 – 3⅞" squares, cut once on the diagonal

From the blue fabric, cut:
2 – 1¼" × 7⅝" rectangles
2 – 1¼" × 9" rectangles

From the red fabric, cut:
1 – 5½" square

Sewing the Block:

1. Draw a line on the diagonal of 2 – 2⅜" light squares. Cut the remaining 4 – 2⅜" light squares once on the diagonal.

2. Putting the right sides together, match a 2⅜" light square and a 2⅜" brown square. Sew ¼" on both sides of the drawn line. Cut apart on the drawn line. Press the seam toward the brown. Square to 2". Make 4.

3. Sew 2 small light triangles from step 1 and the unit from step 2 together. Press the seams toward the light. Make 4.

4. Sew 1 unit from step 3 and a gold triangle together. Press the seam toward the gold. Square to 3½". Make 4.

5. Sew 2 medium light triangles to the unit from step 4. Press the seams toward the light. Make 4.

6. Sew a large light triangle to each side of a 5½" red square. Press the seams toward the light. Square to 7⅝".

7. Sew a 1¼" × 7⅝" blue rectangle to opposite sides of the unit from step 6. Press the seams toward the blue.

GRANDMOTHER'S CROSS

Alma's children, Brenda, Billy and Belinda. Easter in the mid 1950's.

8. Sew a 1¼" × 9" blue rectangle to opposite sides of the previous unit. Press the seams toward the blue. Square to 9".

9. Sew a unit from step 5 to each side of the unit from step 8. Press the seams toward the center. Square to 12½".

Cutting Instructions:

From the light fabric, cut:
2 − 3⅞" squares, cut once on the diagonal
1 − 7¼" square, cut twice on the diagonal
2 − 2⅝" squares

From gold fabric, cut:
8 − 2⅝" squares

From EACH of 2 different red, blue, brown, orange and green fabrics, cut:
1 − 2⅝" square

Sewing the Block:

1. Sew a 2⅝" light square and a 2⅝" orange square together. Press the seam toward the orange. Make 2.

3. Sew 4 – four-patches together to form the block. Press the seams to one side. Square to 8½". Make 2.

4. Sew a 4 flying geese unit to the bottom of one of the units from step 3. Press the seam toward the geese unit.

5. Sew a 6 flying geese unit to the unit from step 4. Press the seam toward the geese unit. Square to 12½". Make 2.

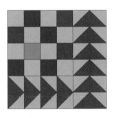

32 PATCH/GEESE BLOCK

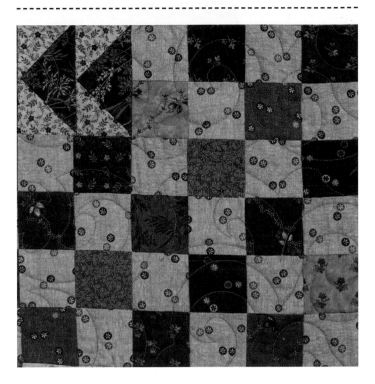

Cutting Instructions for 4 Blocks:

From the green, blue, red, orange, gold and brown fabrics (a total of):
64 – 2½" squares

From the light fabric:
64 – 2½" squares

Sewing the Block:

1. Sew a 2½" dark square and a 2½" light square together. Press the seam toward the dark. Make 64.

2. Sew 2 of the units from step 1 together to form a square. Press the seam to one side. Square to 4½". Make 32.

3. Sew 2 – four-patch units and a 2 flying geese unit together. Press the seam toward the center. Make 4.

Portrait of a Lady ✦ **27** ✦

4. Sew 3 – four-patch units together. Press the seams away from the center. Make 8.

5. Sew 1 row from step 3 and 2 rows from step 4 together to form the block. Press the seams to one side. Square to 12½". Make 4 blocks.

PUTTING THE QUILT TOGETHER

---

1. Referring to the quilt diagram, arrange and sew the blocks into 4 rows. Press according to the arrows.

2. Sew the 4 rows together. Press the rows as indicated below.

ADDING THE BORDERS

Inner Border and Flying Geese Borders Cutting Instructions:

From the green fabric:
6 – 1½" × width of fabric strips
8 – 2¼" × width of fabric strips (reserve for binding)

From EACH of the 2 green, blue, red, orange, gold and brown fabrics:
4 – 2½" × 4½" rectangles

From the light fabric:
96 – 2½" squares

Adding the Inner Border:

1. Sew the 1½" inner border strips together along the short ends. Press the seams to one side.

2. Measure the quilt from left to right through the center. Cut two strips to this measurement. Mark the center of the quilt top and bottom and the center of the border strips. Match the marked centers and pin the borders to the quilt top and bottom. Sew to the quilt. Press the seams toward the borders.

3. Draw a line on the diagonal of the 96 – 2½" light squares. Sew, on the drawn line, a 2½" light square to a 2½" × 4½" dark rectangle. Press the seam toward the light. Trim ¼" from the sewn line. Make 48.

4. Sew, on the drawn line, 1 – 2½" light square to the other side of the previous unit. Press the seam toward the light. Trim ¼" from the sewn line.

5. Sew 24 geese units together to form a row. Press the seams toward the dark. Make 2.

6. Mark the center of the quilt top and bottom and the center of the geese rows. Match the marked centers and pin the rows to the quilt top and bottom. Sew to the quilt. Press the seams toward the dark strip borders.

7. Measure the quilt from left to right through the center. Cut two of the 1½" strips to this measurement. Mark the center of the quilt top and bottom and the center of the border strips. Match the marked centers and pin the borders to the quilt top and bottom. Sew to the quilt. Press the seams toward the borders.

Outer Border Cutting Instructions:

From the red fabric:
36 – 3½" squares, draw a line on the diagonal
2 – 3⅞" squares, draw a line on the diagonal
18 – 2⅝" × 11⅞" rectangles

From the light fabric:
4 – 3½" squares
22 – 3½" × 6½" rectangles
18 – 3⅞" squares, cut once on the diagonal

From the blue fabric:
2 – 3⅞" squares
4 – 3½" × 9½" rectangles
36 – 3½" × 6⅞" rectangles
40 – 3½" × 6½" rectangles

Sewing the Corner Blocks:

1. Putting right sides together, match a 3⅞" red square and a 3⅞" blue square. Sew ¼" on both sides of the drawn line. Cut apart on drawn line. Press the seam toward the blue. Make 4.

2. Sew a 3½" light square to the units from step 1. Press the seam toward the light.

3. Sew a 3½" × 6½" light rectangle to the unit from step 2. Press the seam toward the light.

4. Sew a 3½" × 6½" blue rectangle to the unit from step 3. Press the seam toward the blue.

5. Sew a 3½" × 9½" blue rectangle to the unit from step 4. Press the seam away from the blue. Square to 9½". Make 4.

Sewing the Side Blocks:

1. Sew a light triangle and a 3½" × 6⅞" blue rectangle together. Press the seam open. Using the light triangle as a guide, trim the blue corner off. Make 36.

2. Sew the units from step 1 to both sides of a 2⅝" × 11⅞" red rectangle. Line up the tip of the unit from step 1 and the corner of the red rectangle. Press the seams toward the red. Trim the red corners off using the sides as a guide. Make 18.

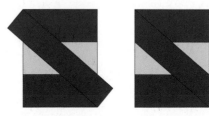

3. Sew, on the drawn line, a 3½" red square and a 3½" × 6½" blue rectangle together. Press the seam toward the red. Make 36.

4. Sew 2 of the units from step 3 to each side of a 3½" × 6½" light rectangle. Press the seams away from the light. Make 18.

5. Sew a unit from steps 2 and 4 together. Press the seam to one side. Square to 12½" × 9½". Make 18.

Adding the Outer Border:

1. Sew 5 side border blocks together. Press the seams to one side. Make 2.

2. Sew 1 to each side of the quilt top. Press the seams toward the borders.

3. Sew 4 side border blocks and 2 corner border blocks together. Press the seams toward the center. Make 2.

4. Sew 1 to the top and bottom of the quilt. Press the seams toward the borders.

FINISHING THE QUILT

----

1. Quilt as desired.

2. Sew the 2¼" green binding strips together along the short ends. Press the seams open. Attach to the quilt.

Enjoy your quilt!

2. Putting the right sides of the fabric together, match a 3½" light square with a 3½" dark square. Sew ¼" on both sides of the drawn line. Cut apart on the drawn line. Press the seams toward the dark. Make 15 from each of the 8 fabrics. You will have 1 extra unit from each color.

3. Sew 2 light tan triangles to the previous units. Press the seams toward the light.

4. Sew a dark triangle to the units from Step 3. Press the seam toward the dark side.

5. Sew 1 − 3⅛" light strip to 1 − 3⅛" purple strip. Make 6. Sub-cut these into 120 − 2" × 5¾" units.

6. Sew 2 units from step 4 and 1 unit from step 5 together to form a top row. Press the A rows toward the center and the B rows away from the center. Make 15 A and 15 B rows.

7. Sew 2 units from step 4 and 1 unit from step 5 together to form a bottom row. Press the A rows toward the center and the B rows away from the center. Make 15 A and 15 B rows.

8. Sew 2 units from step 5 and a 2" purple square together to make a center row. Press the seams toward the light. Make 30.

9. Sew 1 row from steps 6 and 7, and 1 row from step 8 together to form the block. Press the A blocks away from the center and the B blocks toward the center. Make 15 A and 15 B blocks. Square to 12½".

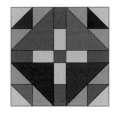

PUTTING THE QUILT TOGETHER

1. Referring to the quilt diagram, arrange (alternating the A and the B blocks) and sew the blocks into 6 rows of 5 blocks each. Press the even number rows to the left and the odd number rows to the right.

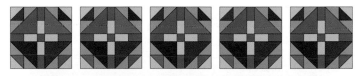

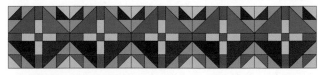

2. Sew the 6 rows together. Press the seams away from the center.

ADDING THE BORDERS

Inner Border:

1. Sew the 2½" green strips together along the short ends. Press the seams to one side.

2. Measure the quilt from the top to the bottom through the center. Cut two strips to this measurement. Mark the center of the quilt sides and the center of the border strips. Match the marked centers and pin the borders to the quilt sides. Sew to the quilt. Press the seams toward the borders.

3. Measure the quilt from left to right, including the already attached borders. Cut two strips to this measurement. Mark the center of the quilt top and bottom and the center of the border strips. Match the marked centers and pin the borders to the quilt top and bottom. Sew to the quilt. Press the seams toward borders.

Outer Border:

1. Sew the 6½" burgundy strips together along the short ends. Press the seams to one side.

2. Measure the quilt from the top to the bottom through the center. Cut two strips to this measurement. Mark the center of the quilt sides and the center of the border strips. Match the marked centers and pin the borders to the quilt sides. Sew to the quilt. Press the seams toward the borders.

3. Measure the quilt from left to right, including the already attached borders. Cut two strips to this measurement. Mark the center of the quilt top and bottom and the center of the border strips. Match the marked centers and pin the borders to the quilt top and bottom. Sew to the quilt. Press the seams toward the borders.

FINISHING THE QUILT

1. Quilt as desired.

2. Sew the 2¼" blue star binding strips together along the short ends. Press the seams open. Attach to the quilt.

Enjoy your quilt!

Sewing the Blocks:

1. Sew a 2" gold/green square B and a 2" light square A together. Press the seam toward the gold/green. Make 48.

2. Sew a 2" × 3½" light rectangle C and the unit from step 1 together. Press the seam toward the light.

Sew a light triangle E to 2 sides of a 2⅝" green/gold square D. Press the seams toward the light. Make 32.

4. At this point you will want to lay out your block for color placement as in Block Diagram on page 40. For 8 of the blocks you will need 2 of the green units from step 3 and 3 of the gold units from step 2 per block. For the other 8 blocks you will use 2 of the gold units from step 3 and 3 of the green units from step 2 per block.

5. Sew a dark triangle F to the right side of the unit from step 3. Press the seam toward the dark. Make 2.

6. Sew a dark triangle G to the left side of the unit. Press the seam toward the dark. Make 2.

7. Sew 2 units from step 2 and a unit from step 6 together to form a row. Press the seams toward the center.

8. Sew a unit from step 2 and a unit from step 6 together to form a row. Press the seam away from the square unit.

9. Sew a dark triangle F and a dark triangle K together. Press the seam open. Repeat with dark triangles G and H, then I and J.

10. Sew 2 units from step 9 and a dark triangle together as in the diagram below. Press the seams away from the center.

11. Sew a unit from step 9 and 2 dark triangles together as in the diagram below. Press the seams toward the triangles.

12. Sew the units from steps 10 and 11 together. Press the seam toward the triangle unit.

13. On the 4⅞" × 7⅜" rectangle L Base, mark the center on one of the 4⅞" sides. From that mark cut diagonally to the corners.

14. Put 2 – 3½" × 10⅝" light rectangles M wrong sides together. Along the 10⅝" side mark 3½" in. From that mark cut diagonally to the corners.

15. Using a scant ¼" seam allowance sew the cut pieces from steps 13 and 14 together. Press the seams toward the light.

16. Sew the units from steps 12 and 15 together. Press the seam toward the unit from step 15.

17. Sew the units from steps 8 and 16 together. Press the seam away from the unit from step 16.

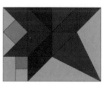

18. Sew the units from steps 7 and 17 together. Press the seam toward the center. Square to 12½".

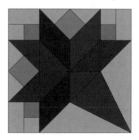

PUTTING THE QUILT TOGETHER

---

1. Referring to the quilt diagram, arrange and sew the blocks into 4 rows of 4 blocks. Press the even number rows to the left and the odd number rows to the right.

2. Sew the 4 rows together. Press the rows away from the center.

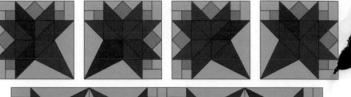

ADDING THE BORDERS

Inner Border:

1. Sew the 2½" red inner border strips together along the short ends. Press the seams to one side.

2. Measure the quilt from left to right through the center. Cut two strips to this measurement. Mark the center of the quilt top and bottom and the center of the border strips. Match the marked centers and pin the borders to the quilt top and bottom. Sew to the quilt. Press the seams toward the borders.

3. Sew a 2½" light square and a 2½" dark square together. Press the seam toward the dark. Sew 2 units together. Press the seam to one side. Make 24.

4. Sew 12 – four-patch units together to form a row. Press the seams to one side. Make 2.

5. Mark the center of the quilt top and bottom and the center of the four-patch rows. Match the marked centers and pin the rows to the quilt top and bottom. Sew to the quilt. Press the seams toward the red borders.

6. Measure the quilt from the top to the bottom through the center. Cut two of the 2½" red strips to this measurement. Mark the center of the quilt sides and the center of the border strips. Match the marked centers and pin the borders to the quilt sides. Sew to the quilt. Press the seams toward the borders.

7. Measure the quilt from left to right, including the already attached borders. Cut two strips to this measurement. Mark the center of the quilt top and bottom and the center of the border strips. Match the marked centers and pin the borders to the quilt top and bottom. Sew to the quilt. Press the seams toward the borders.

Outer Border:

1. Sew the 6½" purple floral strips together along short ends. Press seams to one side.

2. Measure the quilt from the top to the bottom through the center. Cut two strips to this measurement. Mark the center of the quilt sides and the center of the border strips. Match the marked centers and pin the borders to the quilt sides. Sew to the quilt. Press the seams toward the borders.

3. Measure the quilt from left to right, including the already attached borders. Cut two strips to this measurement. Mark the center of the quilt top and bottom and the center of the border strips. Match the marked centers and pin the borders to the ~~...~~

FINISHING THE QUILT

----

1. Quilt as desired.

2. Sew the 2¼" green binding strips together along the short ends. Press the seams open. Attach to the quilt.

Enjoy your quilt!

"Grandma's heart is █████████████

—*Author Unknown*

4. Sew a light A triangle to a brown/blue four-patch unit. Press the seam toward the light. Make 2.

5. Sew 2 light B triangles to the sides of the units in step 4. Press the seams toward the light.

6. Sew 2 brown/blue four-patch units from step 3 to both sides of 1 four-patch unit from step 2. Press the seams toward the center four-patch.

7. Sew 2 light A triangles to the above unit. Press the seams toward the light.

8. Sew the 2 units from step 5 and the unit from step 7 together. Press the seams away from the center. Square to 12½". Repeat to make a total of 3 blocks.

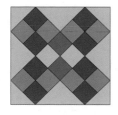

PUTTING THE TABLE RUNNER TOGETHER

1. Referring to the table runner diagram, sew the blocks together to form a row. Press away from the center.

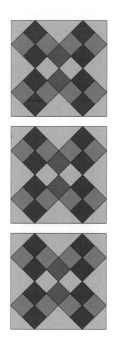

ADDING THE BORDERS

Inner Border:

1. Measure the table runner from the top to the bottom through the center. Cut 2 – 2" stripe strips to this measurement. Mark the center of the table runner sides and the center of the border strips. Match the marked centers and pin the borders to the table runner sides. Sew to the table runner. Press the seams toward the borders.

2. Measure the table runner from left to right, including the already attached borders. Cut 2 – 2" stripe strips to this measurement. Mark the center of the table runner top and bottom and the center of the border strips. Match the marked centers and pin the borders to the table runner top and bottom. Sew to the table runner. Press the seams toward the borders.

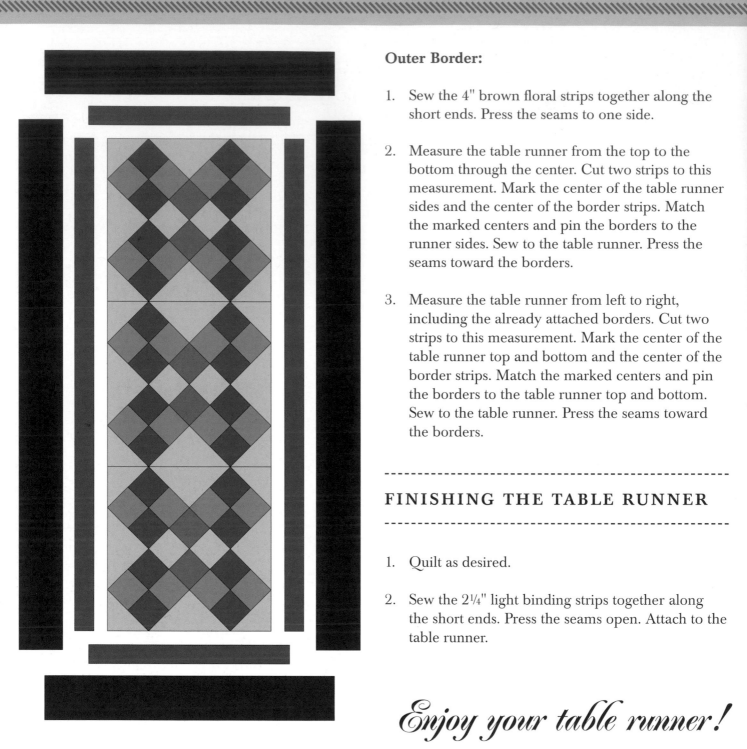

Outer Border:

1. Sew the 4" brown floral strips together along the short ends. Press the seams to one side.

2. Measure the table runner from the top to the bottom through the center. Cut two strips to this measurement. Mark the center of the table runner sides and the center of the border strips. Match the marked centers and pin the borders to the runner sides. Sew to the table runner. Press the seams toward the borders.

3. Measure the table runner from left to right, including the already attached borders. Cut two strips to this measurement. Mark the center of the table runner top and bottom and the center of the border strips. Match the marked centers and pin the borders to the table runner top and bottom. Sew to the table runner. Press the seams toward the borders.

FINISHING THE TABLE RUNNER

----

1. Quilt as desired.

2. Sew the 2¼" light binding strips together along the short ends. Press the seams open. Attach to the table runner.

Enjoy your table runner!

3. Sew 2 light #2 triangles to the previous unit. Press the seams toward the light. Make 80.

4. Sew 1 unit from step 3 and 1 fabric #6 triangle together. Press the seam toward the dark. Square to 3½". Make 80.

5. Sew 2 light #3 triangles to the previous unit. Press the seams toward the light. Make 80.

6. Sew a light #4 triangle to each side of a 5½" #6 square. Press the seams toward the light. Square to 7⅝". Make 20.

7. Sew a 1¼" × 7⅝" gold #5 rectangle to opposite sides of the unit from step 6. Press the seams toward the gold.

8. Sew a 1¼" × 9" gold #5 rectangle to opposite sides of the unit from step 7. Press the seams toward the gold. Square to 9".

9. Sew a unit from step 5 to each side of a unit from step 8. Press the seams toward the center. Square to 12½". Make 20 blocks.

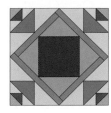

PUTTING THE QUILT TOGETHER

1. Referring to the quilt diagram, arrange and sew the blocks into 5 rows of 4 blocks. Press the even number rows to the left and the odd number rows to the right.

2. Sew the 4 rows together. Press the seams away from the center.

ADDING THE BORDERS

Inner Border:

1. Sew the 2½" green strips together along the short ends. Press the seams to one side.

2. Measure the quilt from the top to the bottom through the center. Cut two strips to this measurement. Mark the center of the quilt sides and the center of the border strips. Match the marked centers and pin the borders to the quilt sides. Sew to the quilt. Press the seams toward the borders.

3. Measure the quilt from left to right, including the already attached borders. Cut two strips to this measurement. Mark the center of the quilt top and bottom and the center of the border strips. Match the marked centers and pin the borders to the quilt top and bottom. Sew to the quilt. Press the seams toward the borders.

Outer Border:

1. Sew the 6½" brown strips together along the short ends. Press the seams to one side.

2. Measure the quilt from the top to the bottom through the center. Cut two strips to this measurement. Mark the center of the quilt sides and the center of the border strips. Match the marked centers and pin the borders to the quilt sides. Sew to the quilt. Press the seams toward the borders.

3. Measure the quilt from left to right, including the already attached borders. Cut two strips to this measurement. Mark the center of the quilt top and bottom and the center of the border strips. Match the marked centers and pin the borders to the quilt top and bottom. Sew to the quilt. Press the seams toward the borders.

FINISHING THE QUILT

1. Quilt as desired.

2. Sew the 2¼" burgundy binding strips together along the short ends. Press the seams open. Attach to the quilt.

Enjoy your quilt!

Sewing the Blocks:

1. Sew a D light triangle to 2 sides of an A dark triangle. Press the seams toward the light.

2. Sew 2 – 2" × 12½" dark rectangles C together. Press the seam to one side.

3. Sew an E light triangle to 2 sides of a B dark triangle. Press the seams toward the light. Make 2.

4. Sew 2 of the units together from step 3. Press the seam open.

5. Sew the units from steps 1, 2 and 4 together to form a block. Press the seams toward the center. Square to 12½". Make 2 heart blocks.

HOUSE BLOCKS

Cutting Instructions for 2 Blocks:

From the light fabric, cut:
4 – 3½" × 5½" rectangles
2 – 1½" × 2½" rectangles
4 – 3½" squares, draw a line on the diagonal

From each of 2 fabrics (door/windows), cut:
1 – 2½" × 4½" rectangle
2 – 2" × 2½" rectangles

From each of 2 fabrics (chimney), cut:
1 – 2½" square

From each of 2 fabrics (roof), cut:
1 – 3½" square, draw a line on the diagonal
1 – 3½" × 6½" rectangle

From each of 2 fabrics (house), cut:
3 – 1½" × 2½" rectangles
3 – 2½" × 6½" rectangles
2 – 2½" × 4½" rectangles
1 – 3½" × 6½" rectangle

Sewing the Blocks:

1. Sew a 1½" × 2½" light rectangle and a 2½" chimney square together. Press the seam toward the dark.

2. Sew a 3½" × 5½" light rectangle to each side of the previous unit. Press the seams toward the light.

3. Sew, on drawn line, a 3½" light square to the left end of a 3½" × 6½" house rectangle. Press the seam toward the light. Trim ¼" from the sewn line.

4. Sew, on drawn line, a 3½" roof square to the right end of the previous unit. Press the seam toward the roof triangle. Trim ¼" from the sewn line.

5. Sew a 2½" × 4½" house rectangle to each side of a 2½" × 4½" door rectangle. Press the seams toward the door rectangle.

6. Sew the previous units and a 2½" × 6½" house rectangle together. Press the seams toward the house rectangle.

7. Sew, on drawn line, a 3½" light square to the right end of a 3½" × 6½" roof rectangle. Press the seam toward the light. Trim ¼" from the sewn line.

8. Sew 2 – 2" × 2½" window rectangles and 3 – 1½" × 2½" house rectangles together. Press the seams toward the window rectangles.

9. Sew 2 – 2½" × 6½" house rectangles and the units from steps 7 and 8 together. Press the seams away from the house rectangles.

10. Sew the units from steps 6 and 9 together. Press the seam to one side.

11. Sew the unit from step 2 to the above unit. Press the seam away from the house. Square to 12½". Make 2 house blocks.

SASHING/CORNER STONE'S/ PIANO KEY BORDER/BINDING

Cutting Instructions:

From the light print fabric, cut:
2 – 2⅞" squares, cut once on the diagonal
4 – 2½" × 4⅞" rectangles
4 – 2½" × 6⅞" rectangles
30 – 2½" × 6½" rectangles

From the light fabric, cut:
1 – 2½" square

From the blue fabric, cut:
4 – 2½" × 12½" rectangles
4 – 2½" × width of fabric strips

From the assorted dark fabrics, cut:
2 – 2⅞" squares, cut once on the diagonal
4 – 2½" × 4⅞" rectangles
4 – 2½" × 6⅞" rectangles
30 – 2½" × 6½" rectangles

From the green fabric, cut:
5 – 2¼" × width of fabric strips

PUTTING THE WALL HANGING TOGETHER

----

1. Referring to the wall hanging diagram, sew the blocks and the sashing strips together to form 2 rows. Press the seams toward the sashing strips.

2. Sew 2 – 2½" × 12½" blue strips and 1 – 2½" light square together to form a sashing row. Press the seams toward the blue strips.

3. Sew the rows together, alternating the block rows and the sashing row. Press the seams toward the sashing strips.

ADDING BORDERS

Inner Border:

1. Measure the wall hanging from the top to the bottom through the center. Cut 2 – 2½" blue strips to this measurement. Mark the center of the wall

hanging sides and the center of the border strips. Match the marked centers and pin the borders to the wall hanging sides. Sew to the wall hanging. Press the seams toward the borders.

2. Measure the wall hanging from left to right, including the already attached borders. Cut 2 – 2½" blue strips to this measurement. Mark the center of the wall hanging top and bottom and the center of the border strips. Match the marked centers and pin the borders to the wall hanging top and bottom. Sew to the wall hanging. Press the seams toward the borders.

Outer Border:

1. Sew a dark triangle, a 2½" × 4⅞" light rectangle and a 2½" × 6⅞" dark rectangle together. Press the seams toward the dark. Using the triangle as a guide, cut off the corners of the rectangles. Make 2 of each.

2. Sew a light triangle, a 2½" × 4⅞" dark rectangle and a 2½" × 6⅞" light rectangle together. Press the seams toward the dark. Using the triangle as a guide, cut off the corners of the rectangles. Make 2 of each.

3. Sew 2 of the previous units together. Press the seam to one side. Square to 6½". Make 2 of each.

4. Sew 7 – 2½" × 6½" light rectangles and 8 – 2½" × 6½" dark rectangles together, alternating the two. Press the seams to one side. Make 2.

5. Sew the strip sets to the sides of the wall hanging. Press the seams toward the center.

6. Sew 8 – 2½" × 6½" light rectangles and 7 – 2½" × 6½" dark rectangles together, alternating the two. Press the seams to one side. Make 2. Sew 1 corner block to each end. Press the seams away from the center.

7. Sew the strip sets to the top and the bottom of the wall hanging. Press the seams toward the center.

FINISHING THE WALL HANGING

---

1. Quilt as desired.

2. Sew the 2¼" green binding strips together along the short ends. Press the seams open. Attach to the wall hanging.

Enjoy your wall hanging!